D-DAY

Turning Points in American History

D-DAY

Marilyn Miller

Silver Burdett Company, Morristown, New Jersey

Cincinnati; Glenview, Ill.; San Carlos, Calif.;
Dallas; Atlanta; Agincourt, Ontario

Acknowledgments

We would like to thank the following people for reviewing the manuscript and for their guidance and helpful suggestions: David Williams, Professor of History, California State University; Craighton Hippenhammer, Assistant Coordinator and Children's Service Manager, Cuyahoga County Public Library, Cleveland, Ohio; and Vincent J. Coffey.

Maps by Betsy Blackwell

All illustrations courtesy of the United States Department of the Army unless otherwise specified.

Library of Congress Cataloging-in-Publication Data

Miller, Marilyn, 1946-
  D-Day

  (Turning.points in American history)
  Bibliography: p.
  Includes index.
  Summary: Trace the events of the Allied invasion
of German-occupied France from the beaches of Normandy
which took place on June 6, 1944.
    1. World War, 1939-1945--Campaigns--France--
Normandy--Juvenile literature. 2. Normandy (France)--
History--Juvenile literature. [1. World War, 1939-
1945--Campaigns--France--Normandy. 2. Normandy
(France)--History] I.Title. II. Series.

D756.5.N6M48   1986   940.54'21   8440380
ISBN 0-382-06825-4 (lib. bdg.)
ISBN 0-382-06972-2 (pbk.)

 Created by Media Projects Incorporated

Series design by Bruce Glassman
Ellen Coffey, Project Editor
Charlotte McGuinn Freeman, Associate Editor, Photo Research Editor
Michael A. Wong, Editorial Associate
Bernard Schleifer, Design Consultant

CONTENTS

INTRODUCTION

EISENHOWER'S DECISION

It was just before dawn on the morning of June 4, 1944. The starry sky was good news. It signaled clear weather, which meant the invasion could proceed as planned. Europe had been at war since 1939, the United States since 1941, when Germany's Axis ally, Japan, attacked our Army and Naval bases at Pearl Harbor. During those years of war there had been fighting on land and sea in the Pacific, in Africa, and in Asia. Russian armies faced the Germans in the East. But except in Italy, no English or American army fought on the continent of Europe. General Dwight D. Eisenhower, his jeep speeding across the dark English countryside, looked up at the stars shining in the clear night sky. The General was traveling to South-wick House, the Supreme Headquarters for the Allied Expeditionary Force (SHAEF). The Allied armies were to invade France at last. D-Day, the day of invasion, was finally at hand.

British Prime Minister Winston S. Churchill, General Eisenhower, and Brigadier General Maxwell D. Taylor review the 101st Airborne Division, two weeks before the scheduled invasion.

General Eisenhower, Supreme Commander of the Allied Forces in Europe, was scheduled to meet with his staff. This group included the top military officers of Great Britain, the United States, and Canada, which had joined forces to fight Germany, Italy, and Japan. Also among the Allies were armed forces of France and Poland that had escaped from Europe when those countries fell to the Germans. There were also the forces of the French "Resistance" movement, operating within France to aid the Allied forces and to sabotage German operations in their country.

The Allied High Command for the invasion was an unprecedented partnership. Each branch of the headquarters had a commander of one nationality and a deputy of the other, thus insuring minimal friction as the planning had proceeded. General Eisenhower was assisted by Americans Lieutenant-General W. Beddell Smith, Chief of Staff of Supreme Command, and Lieutenant-General Omar Bradley, Commander of the First U.S. Army. The British High Command personnel included Air Chief Marshal Sir Arthur Tedder, Deputy Supreme Commander; General Sir Bernard L. Montgomery, Land Commander; Admiral Sir Bertram Ramsey, Naval Commander; and Sir Trafford Leigh-Mallory, Air Chief Marshal. But the final responsibility for the invasion was Eisenhower's alone.

The officers of the Allied High Command listened attentively to a report from the Chief Meteorologist, British Group Captain T.M. Stagg. He informed them that although the dawn outside the windows of Southwick House looked fine, the morning would not long remain so. A low pressure system, Stagg reported, was moving toward the French coast. The incoming storm was due to strike the beaches at Normandy on the northwest coast of France, the site of the planned invasion, sometime early the next morning. This storm carried with it winds that would reach speeds of forty-five miles per hour.

A landing in such weather would be a disaster. General Eisenhower thought it over for only a moment before giving the order to postpone. They would hold off another twenty-four hours, and hope for the best.

They knew they could not wait long, for there would be only three days during which other conditions crucial to the success of the invasion would prevail. In addition to the weather, the phase of the moon and the tides had to be ideal for the assault.

The moon had to be full, to provide sufficient light for the pilots of the gliders to spot the targeted landing zones. The pilots of the paratroop transports would need light, too, to find the "drop zones." And with the light of the full moon, the paratroopers, once safely on the ground, could more easily link up with each other to form effective fighting units behind the enemy lines.

The tide had to be at its lowest ebb, for along that particular stretch of coastline the water level rises twenty-one feet between low and high tides. A low tide was essential if the landing craft were to avoid the large metal, concrete, and wooden obstacles the Allies knew had been placed in the water just off the French beaches under the orders of German General Erwin Rommel—obstacles such as large metal spikes protruding upwards from the sand, with explosive mines atop them. A low tide was essential, too, so that a wide expanse of beach was exposed, allowing the landing of many men and their equipment without the men being at risk of drowning or the vehicles of being swamped in high water.

Clear weather was necessary to prevent confusion among the large number of troops and units trying to land. The smaller landing craft that had been devised for this invasion, when loaded with a platoon of troops carrying heavy equipment, rode very low in the water. The Dual Drive Tanks (DD's) were powered by a propeller system while in the water, and could be switched over to an ordinary track propulsion system (like that on a standard tank) once on land.

These were some of the factors General Eisenhower had to take into account along with Captain Stagg's weather report. That night Eisenhower had to postpone the

American Generals at 12th Army Headquarters. (Front row, left to right) Lieutenant General William H. Simpson; General George S. Patton; General Carl A. Spaatz; General Dwight D. Eisenhower, Supreme Allied Commander; General Omar N. Bradley; General Courtney H. Hodges; Lieutenant General Leonard T. Gerow. (Back row, left to right) Brigadier General Ralph F. Stearky; Lieutenant General Hoyt S. Vandenberg; Lieutenant General Walter G. Smith, Chief of Staff, SHAEF; Major General Otto P. Weiland; Brigadier General Richard E. Nugent.

invasion for at least twenty-four hours, or face certain defeat and the loss of many men. The invasion, however, could not be postponed for long. By an elaborate plan of deception, maintained with tight security measures, the Allies had made sure that the Germans were still unaware of the specific invasion site. A longer postponement would endanger the secrecy of the plan. The fate of the invasion, and of Europe, were at stake.

When Eisenhower arrived at Headquarters the next morning, Southwick House was shaking from the force of the storm that raged, as predicted, across the English Channel—the moat separating the coast of England from what Hitler had designated his *Festung Europa,* "Fortress Europe." Again, the Allied Chiefs of Staff met in the War Room. On this morning, however, Captain Stagg was attempting to restrain a smile. He had better news for the Supreme Commander. The storm would break, and there would be relatively clearer skies for a period of twenty-four to thirty-six hours, beginning sometime around midnight that night, June fifth.

This break in the weather would make the invasion just barely possible. But it would not leave much time to land the support troops and supplies necessary to hold the captured shoreline. In order for the invasion to succeed, the Allied forces would have to carry out their plans quickly.

At last Eisenhower gave the order to proceed with the invasion. His aides hurriedly left the War Room, to translate Eisenhower's order into the innumerable actions that would become the invasion. The Supreme Commander, now alone, wrote out the following message, to be released only if the invasion failed:

Our landings in the Cherbourg-Havre area have failed to gain a satisfactory foothold and I have withdrawn the troops. My decision to attack at this time and place was based upon the best information available. The troops, the Air and the Navy did all that bravery and devotion could do. If any blame or fault attaches to the attempt it is mine alone. June 5, 1944.

FINLAND

NORWAY   SWEDEN

Leningrad

ESTONIA

BALTIC
SEA

NORTH SEA

LATVIA

DENMARK

LITHUANIA

Schleswig

Danzig (Free City)

IRELAND

EAST
PRUSSIA

UNITED
KINGDOM

NETHERLANDS

Berlin

USSR

Warsaw

London

BELGIUM

GERMANY

POLAND

ATLANTIC
OCEAN

Bonn

Silesia

Paris

Saar

Prague

FRANCE

CZECHOSLOVAKIA

Vienna

SWITZERLAND

AUSTRIA

Odenburg

HUNGARY

RUMANIA

Klagenfurt

TRENTINO

YUGOSLAVIA

BLACK
SEA

SPAIN

ITALY

BULGARIA

ALBANIA

MEDITERRANEAN SEA

GREECE

TURKEY

EUROPE AFTER VERSAILLES

1919

PLEBISCITE AREAS

THE WORLD
AT WAR AGAIN

The attempts of Germany to dominate Europe, which eventually led to two World Wars, began when the "states" of Germany were unified under Prussian leadership in 1870. This unification had been accomplished by means of authoritarianism and militarism. The demands and conquests of a powerful united Germany resulted in a divided Europe, as the other major and minor powers allied themselves with or against Germany. The nations of Europe were thus divided into two armed camps.

The Austrian Archduke Ferdinand was assassinated in August, 1914. The nations of Europe, divided by their entangling set of alliances, were pitched into war.

This conflict would eventually be referred to as World War I, but before the outbreak of what would become World War II, it was called, simply, "The Great War." Much of World War I was fought along "the Western Front," a line of trenches that stretched the length of the European continent from the North Sea to Switzer-

land. For four years the opposing forces tried, with great loss of life and little success, to break through these entrenched lines. Just as the German forces seemed ready at last to burst through the battered British and French defenses, America entered the war. With the support of American troops and equipment, the allied British and French forces were able to stop the German advance, to counter-attack, and eventually to force a collapse of the morale of the German troops. Germany's opponents had won The Great War. The loss of life and property had been enormous. It was widely believed that this would be the last Great War—"the war to end all wars." This optimism about world peace, however, proved to be premature.

The people of Germany could not accept their defeat. It had come too quickly, just as they were on the verge of victory. At no time during World War I had the opposing armies fought on German soil. The German people had come to believe that the fighting forces of their nation were invincible. In an effort to understand their defeat, a myth arose among the Germans that their army had been sabotaged by traitors at home.

The Treaty of Versailles, dictated to a defeated Germany by the Allies at the close of the war, was particularly humiliating to the German nation. This document declared (among the many stipulations it contained) that the German government be forced to pay large monetary reparations to their victorious enemies. The treaty forbade the rebuilding of German armed forces. The treaty also forced Germany to return the provinces of Alsace and Lorraine, which it had taken from France in 1870, to French control; to cede control of the Saarland (a German province on the French border) to the government of France until reparations were paid in full; and to provide Poland with a corridor to the sea on the east, which divided German territory. Seen by the German nation as harsh and cruel, these terms of the Treaty of Versailles endangered the very peace in Europe that the treaty was designed to assure.

The worldwide Great Depression of the late 1920s plunged the German economy into ruin. It was in the 1920s that Adolf Hitler, who had been a corporal in the German army during "the Great War," began his rise to power through the newly-formed National Socialist German Workers' Party, known as the Nazi Party. The Nazi Party's anti-democratic, right-wing political platform blamed Germany's defeat in the war on the Socialists, Communists, Democrats, and Jews.

Hitler was jailed in 1924 for attempting to overthrow the German government. During his imprisonment he wrote *Mein Kampf*—a book in which he pledged to the German people that once in power he would reverse the much-loathed Treaty of Versailles, renew the economy, and punish those he claimed had sold out the German nation, especially the Jews. After his release from prison, Hitler consolidated his power in Germany. In 1933 Hitler's authoritarian politics, which preached the racial superiority of the German people, became the policies of the nation.

In 1935, the people of the Saarland voted by referendum to rejoin the German nation. The rich coal and mineral deposits of the Saar region were thus returned to German control. In 1936, Germany remilitarized the Rhineland, another province along Germany's border with France. The other nations of Europe became alarmed at what appeared to be increasing German emphasis on preparing for another war. England and France, however, did nothing. The officials of the British and French governments hoped that Hitler wanted only to rebuild a strong Germany, which they thought might prevent the expansion of Russia. The Russian nation had also grown powerful since its revolution in 1917. Under the leadership of another ruthless dictator, Josef Stalin, Russia was becoming a power feared by many other nations of Europe, even more than Germany.

In March, 1938, Hitler took over Austria. Later that year he demanded the "Sudetanland," the German-speaking provinces of Czechoslovakia. German demands for acquisitions of territory prompted the

British and French heads of government to meet in Munich with Hitler and his Italian Fascist ally, Benito Mussolini. Britain and France agreed to Germany's annexation of the Czechoslovakian provinces, thinking that a policy of appeasement would preserve the peace, for Hitler had declared that this was his last territorial demand in Europe.

In March, 1939, Hitler took the remainder of Czechoslovakia. He then signed a peace treaty with Russia, hoping to avoid a two-front war, the prospect of which he greatly feared. Again, Britain and France stood by, making only verbal protests, while Hitler continued to pursue his goal of German dominance in Europe.

In September, 1939, Hitler invaded Poland. Within three weeks, Poland was crushed by Hitler's *blitzkreig*, the "lightning war" that pitted the crack German air force—the *Luftwaffe*—and the armored or "Panzer" divisions of the German Army—the *Wehrmacht*—against the Polish cavalry. The world was stunned. Hitler's use of coordinated armored and air forces to break quickly through enemy lines was a completely new form of warfare.

Following the invasion of Poland, France and Great Britain declared war on Germany. The Second World War had begun. The Germans were not to be stopped, however. After a period of virtual inactivity, known as the "phony war," in the spring of 1940 Hitler turned his attentions to the West. By the summer of 1940, Hitler's Panzers had conquered Belgium, the Netherlands and France, and the British had evacuated their army from Dunkirk, on the French coast. Hitler had gained control over most of continental Europe. He had even gained a war partner, when armed forces of Mussolini's Italy, another Axis nation, invaded France after the Germans had won the battle.

Beginning in 1940, the Luftwaffe and the British Royal Air Force (known as the RAF) were engaged in heavy fighting in the skies over England. The English held firm during this "Battle of Britain," and the civilian population showed great courage during the nightly German air raids on their cities. In 1941, having failed to destroy the Royal Air Force, which would have made an invasion of Britain possible, Hitler turned his armies to the East. German forces invaded the lands of their former ally, Russia, and succeeded in penetrating almost to the gates of Moscow, some hundreds of miles within Russian territory.

On December 7, 1941, the Axis nation of Japan attacked Pearl Harbor Naval Base in the Hawaiian Islands. The United States declared war on Japan, and Germany declared war on the United States. This proved to be Hitler's worst mistake.

The American military command was concerned about the war in the Pacific, but felt that a policy of "Defeat Germany First" would be best in the long run, because Germany was the strongest of the Axis powers. The American armed forces adopted a plan of defense and containment in the Pacific. At the Battle of Midway, the American Navy destroyed four Japanese aircraft carriers, which brought the Japanese Navy's strength in aircraft carriers down to par with the American. This stalemate in the Pacific left the Americans

U.S. aircraft carrier following an air strike at the Battle of Midway. This was the only U.S. ship lost during the battle.

free to plan a full-scale invasion of the European continent.

The American generals wanted to invade France in 1942, but their British allies convinced them that it could not yet be done. The invasion would require an unprecedented build-up of troops and supplies. At the height of its power, the German Army had been unable to stage an invasion across the English Channel. The British generals felt, therefore, that more time to prepare was essential.

The British and American generals had different views, too, as to the best method of defeating the Axis powers. The British Chiefs of Staff felt that engaging the Germans on a number of fronts, causing them to diffuse their strength around the periphery of Europe and driving them back in a "tightening noose" on Berlin, was the best plan. The American generals felt that

this would waste both time and lives. They wanted to stage a full-scale invasion on the shores of France, and strike directly at the heart of the Nazi empire.

As a compromise, and to give American troops combat experience, the Allied forces mounted a campaign to recapture North Africa from the Italian and German troops. In 1942, the tide began to turn against the Axis powers. The British Eighth Army, under General Sir Bernard Law Montgomery, defeated the German General Erwin Rommel at El Alamein in Egypt. Farther west in North Africa the Americans landed in Morocco and Algeria. The British and American forces linked up to defeat the German *Afrika Corps* in Tunisia.

In the winter of 1942-43, the forces of Russian Marshal Georgi Zhukov surrounded the German Sixth Army at Stalingrad and forced its surrender. Thus began the expulsion of German troops from Russian soil.

Allied forces captured Sicily in August, 1943, and again the Americans pushed for an invasion of France. Russia, now among the Allied nations, was fighting alone on the continent against the German army. The Russians commanders were also pushing for the invasion, hoping it would relieve some of the pressure on the Russian troops by creating a "second front," and dividing the German forces.

In September, 1943, the Allies invaded the mainland of Italy. A portion of the Allied forces was reserved, however, for assignment in England—the build-up of the thousands of troops and tons of equipment essential to the invasion of Normandy, on the French seacoast.

Troop camps were springing up across southwestern England, and American and British soldiers began conducting strange exercises on land and on the beaches. Fields began to resemble huge parking lots, as row upon row of trucks, tanks, airplanes, and the newly-designed jeeps were collected in preparation for the invasion, and stored under camouflage.

As the British and American armies struggled to take the Italian "boot," and the build-up of forces for an invasion of France was underway, the Allies began Operation FORTITUDE, the most extensive and successful plan of deception ever undertaken. The keystone of the plan rested upon con-

"Attack—Invasion Preparation—Slapton Sands—Devon, England." This watercolor painting by Navy artist Dwight C. Shepler shows the invasion troops staging a "trial run" along a deserted stretch of beach on the English coast. In the months prior to D-Day, many such operations were carried out.

vincing the German High Command that the point of invasion was to be the Pas de Calais, and not the Normandy coast. If the plan succeeded, the Germans would concentrate large forces near the Pas de Calais. Thus, the Allied commanders hoped, the actual site of the invasion would be less strongly defended—which would mean a greater chance of success when the assault came.

The Pas de Calais is at the narrowest section of the English Channel, and for centuries has been the easiest crossing point. There were a number of similar ports on the coast of France, all of which the Germans had fortified heavily, since they could not conceive of the Allies invading elsewhere than at a port—which, once captured, could be used to supply the invasion of the continent. The Allies had attempted to invade at the port of Dieppe on the Normandy coast in 1942, and had discovered in a disastrous and bloody battle that it is nearly impossible to capture a heavily fortified port city directly. They had decided, therefore, to invade the European continent from the beaches of Normandy. It was important that the Germans remain convinced, however, that the Allies intended to attempt to capture a port, most likely at the Pas de Calais.

The German Secret Service was receiving reports from its most trusted agents that the invasion at Normandy would be a diversionary operation, intended to distract the Germans from a much larger invasion to come later along the Pas de Calais. The German High Command did not know, of course, that their secret agents were under British control.

The Axis powers could not verify any of the information they were receiving from their British-controlled agents. From the time of the Battle of Britain in 1941, the Royal Air Force had complete air superiority over the German Luftwaffe in the skies over England. When an occasional German plane did get through, its crew observed only what the RAF intended should be seen—row upon row of false troop housing and phony equipment that the Allies had placed near the Pas de Calais to give the impression that troops were massing there for an attack on the continent. The real troops and equipment were off to the south, well camouflaged and busy preparing for the invasion.

The Allies had sea superiority, too. This was a result of the size of the British and American fleets, the most powerful in the world. The Allies had also developed "radar" and "sonar," electronic air and underwater detection devices that enabled them to spot and destroy enemy aircraft and submarines. The Germans had nothing to match the Allies at sea. Thus the Allies were assured of total control of the English Channel, something Hitler had struggled for but had never achieved. The Allied invasion force, therefore, could not be defeated while still at sea.

Operation FORTITUDE was so successful that on the day of the invasion the Allies had the audacity to "leak" the entire plan of attack to the Germans, misinforming them that it was only a diversionary tactic and not the main invasion. The Allied deceptive measures were crucial. They confused the German High Command, causing them to argue among themselves. With this bold deception the Allies bought

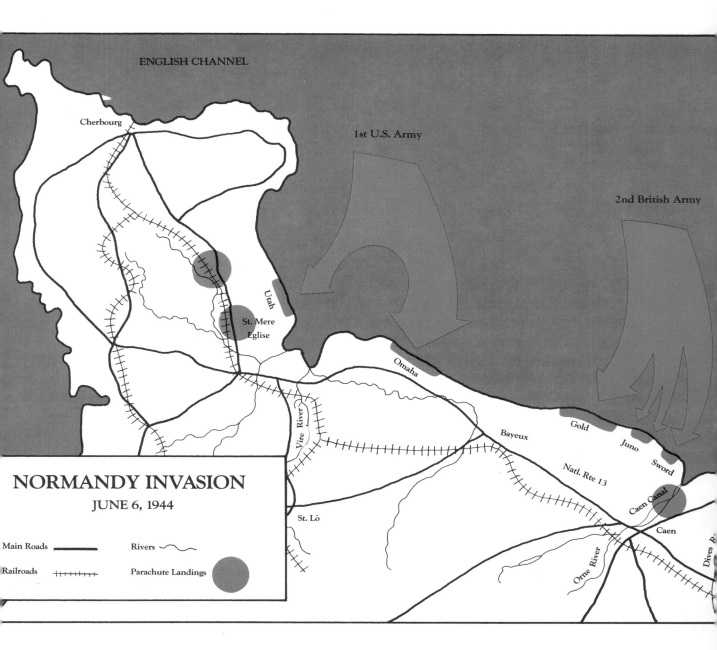

NORMANDY INVASION
JUNE 6, 1944

ENGLISH CHANNEL

Cherbourg

1st U.S. Army

2nd British Army

Utah

St. Mere
Eglise

Omaha

Vire River

Bayeux

Gold

Juno

Sword

Natl. Rte 13

Caen Canal

Caen

St. Lô

Orne River

Dives R.

Main Roads _____   Rivers ～～～

Railroads ++++++++   Parachute Landings ⬤

enough time to land sufficient troops to sustain the invasion before the Germans discovered the actual site.

On June 5, 1944, the years of planning, training, and massing equipment were over. The time for the invasion, code-named OVERLORD, had come at last.

The paratroopers, the first elements of the assault, were boarding transport planes. Each transport towed glider planes loaded with more airborne troops and supplies. Glider pilots and navigators climbed aboard. The squadrons formed in the night skies over England, and winged their way toward France. People all over southern England heard, and watched them go.

2

THE VANGUARD

It was the largest air assault ever mounted in war. Five beaches along the Normandy coast were to be attacked from the sea by British and American, Canadian, Polish, and Free French troops. From west to east these beaches were code-named Utah, Omaha, Gold, Juno and Sword. The forces of the United States First Army were to assault Utah and Omaha beaches, while the British Second Army (which included the Canadian First Army) was to assault Gold, Juno, and Sword. The paratroopers' overall mission was to buy time, to allow the seaborne forces to get ashore in sufficient numbers to meet any German counterthrust. The assault by airborne troops was intended to surprise and confuse the defending Germans.

The paratroopers were to be dropped in two areas across the eastern and west-

General Eisenhower urges the paratroops to "Full Victory—nothing else" as they prepared to board their planes. The blackened faces were an extra camouflage precaution.

ern access routes to the invasion beaches. In the east, many elements of the British Sixth Airborne Division were to be dropped by parachute behind the Sword beachhead. Others were to land with the gliders, carrying heavy supplies in with them. Their mission was to capture the bridges leading into the invasion area.

In the west, the American 101st and 82nd Airborne Divisions (the "Screaming Eagles" and the "All Americans") were also to descend by parachutes and gliders in another, larger area behind the Utah beachhead—the Cotentin Peninsula. Once on the ground, they were to capture the bridges of the rivers Marne and Douve, and the little village of St. Mère Eglise. This would cut off German access to National Route 13, the only major road by which troops and supplies could be transported.

The tactic of dropping paratroopers directly into an invasion area was relatively new. Using this tactic to circumvent "Fortress Holland," the Germans had taken the Netherlands in 1940. That same year,

German paratroopers had invaded Crete over the heads of a powerless British naval force. Despite the many deaths by misadventure, British and American enthusiasm for paratroop landings, and faith in paratroop forces, continued to grow.

The paratroopers, then, were the vanguard in both the literal sense—the troops that lead an army into battle—and in the figurative sense—the leaders of a new trend.

The paratroopers had received the order to go, and were gearing up. These troops were to descend directly into the combat zone, without any of the traditional lines of support and supply behind them. Thus the men had to carry with them everything they might need once they hit the ground behind enemy lines.

A typical paratrooper carried, strapped to his body, a load somewhat like the following:

"One suit of olive drab, worn under my jumpsuit—this was an order for everyone—helmet, boots, gloves, main parachute, Mae West (an inflatable life-vest), rifle, .45 automatic pistol, trench knife, jump knife, hunting knife, machete, one cartridge belt, two bandoliers, two cans of machine-gun ammo, one Hawkins mine, four blocks of TNT, one entrenching tool with two blasting caps taped to the outside, three first-aid kits, two morphine needles, one gas mask, a canteen of water, three days' supply of K rations, two days' supply of D rations, six fragmentation grenades, one Gammon grenade (a lump of plastic explosive in a stocking bag which, when thrown at a tank, would detonate on impact, detaching a "scab" of metal from the tank's armor which would ricochet around the inside of the tank to kill or disable its operators), one orange and one red smoke grenade (for signaling), one orange panel (by which troopers were to be able to recognize each other), one blanket, one raincoat, one change of socks and underwear, two cartons of cigarettes."

A paratroop platoon as a whole had to carry enough equipment to function as a unit once on the ground behind enemy lines. Therefore, some members of the jump group carried such items as blood plasma, rocket launchers callled bazookas, ammunition, radio sets, signal beacons, and the other assorted equipment necessary to launch a preliminary invasion without backup support. These forces had to be able to survive behind enemy lines until the beach invasion succeeded, an event that might take some time and concerning which there was much uncertainty.

The paratroopers were dropped from planes traveling at relatively high speeds. Thus the harness straps had to be extremely tight. Since the troopers' packs were so heavy, the men had great difficulty gearing up, and often had to assist one another. There were reports of soldiers sitting or standing atop one another while a third trooper struggled to fasten the buckles of the harness. Once buckled in, some soldiers had to be hauled to their feet and

A panoramic view of the invasion area.

helped into the transport planes.

On this D-Day, twelve thousand American paratroopers were to be dropped behind enemy lines by over nine hundred troop carrier planes. Another four thousand men would land in five hundred gliders. Commander Eisenhower arrived at the airfield while the men were gearing up. Eisenhower circulated quietly among the busy paratroopers, stopping now and then to ask a man where he was from, another his age, or simply to offer his support and encouragement. The fate of these young paratroopers weighed heavily on the general's mind. As he said in an interview years later, "You know there's going to be losses along the line . . . and goodness knows, those boys meant a lot to me."

Crowded into a transport plane, the paratroopers could ride only on their knees, resting their heavy burdens on the seats behind them. Speech was barely possible over the din of the plane's engines. Some of the paratroopers slept, partly because they had been given double doses of medication to prevent motion sickness. Those who were awake watched the moonlit waters of the English Channel below them, and the companion planes flying in the tight "V" of the formation.

Suddenly an enormous cloud bank was upon them. As the planes entered the cloud mass the pilots instinctively broke formation, as a safety measure. Once out of the cloud bank, some of the planes were miles off course. By this time they had been sighted, and the German ground forces were firing at them. The pilots swerved to avoid the "flak"—anti-aircraft shells bursting in midair. The paratroopers, standing

clipped into the "static" lines above their heads preparatory to the jump, were thrown against the walls and floors of the maneuvering planes.

In an effort to complete their drops before being downed by flak, some pilots dropped their paratroopers at higher speeds than had been designated. As a result, the landing paratroopers were scattered over a very wide area, which made it difficult for them to come together in units, as had been planned. Also, many paratroopers were injured during "opening shock," the jolt a paratrooper experienced when his parachute unfurled while he was moving through the transport plane's "slipstream." This jolt was so severe in many cases that it knocked a trooper unconscious, or resulted in a back injury or injury to a knee or other joint.

When the paratroopers hit the ground, impact claimed many victims. Broken bones were common, especially among the older officers, whose bones were more brittle than those of the young paratroopers. One of these older officers, Lieutenant-Colonel Benjamin Vandevoort, found an abandoned farm cart, from which he led his men into battle despite the broken leg he had sustained on impact.

But it was the low-lying areas that the Germans had flooded, along the Douve and Meredet rivers and just behind the ridge along the beach, that caused the greatest havoc for the landing paratroopers. These flooded areas had not been visible in the aerial photographs taken by Allied reconaissance planes. Paratroopers prepared to land on what they thought was solid ground found themselves in two to three feet of water. Standard landing procedure was to roll upon impact, in order to break the fall. Landing in water, troopers with 100 to 150 pounds of gear strapped to their bodies found themselves tangled in weeds. Often they were unable to cut themselves loose from their billowing parachutes. Many drowned in the shallow water.

The most serious problem facing the surviving paratroopers was the disorientation caused by the inaccurate drops. The maps the troopers carried were useless, for the men were often miles from their assigned drop zones.

Troop concentration was almost impossible, because the men who were to form the units were dropped so far from one another. Even when the drops were accurate, the disorientation caused by opening shock was so complete that the troopers failed to recognize their surroundings. Essential equipment had been ripped away from paratroopers descending at high speeds. Rifles and heavy arms had been lost, as well as signal beacons and radio sets. One typical group, set to rally around a green signal light and to listen for the sound of a large brass cowbell, lost both items during the jump. Some members of the 101st American Airborne Division, the Screaming Eagles, found one another by listening for the clicking sound of little metal "cricket" toys they had carried in their jumpsuit pockets. Unfortunately for some, the sound of the bolt in a German rifle made a similar sound, which led to some nasty surprises.

In the eastern drop zone, the British Sixth Airborne troops had fared better than the Americans. They were dropped with greater accuracy, and had stronger glider support, an equally important factor. The greater the number of gliders that made it safely to the ground in a given assault area, the greater the amount of essential equipment that would be available to the assault troops. The British Sixth Airborne managed to take their objectives—the bridgeheads of the Caen Canal and the mouth of the River Orne—quickly, and with few casualties. Thus these troops had effectively secured the eastern edge of the entire invasion area, and controlled the route north from the city of Caen.

Some of the American paratroopers who had been scattered in the drop zones, unable to link up with their units, found safe hiding places and went to sleep. Drowsiness was a major problem for the paratroopers in the early hours of the invasion. Entire units, sitting down to rest for a moment, found themselves waking up hours later. This strange drowsiness has been attributed to fatigue, nervous tension, and the after-effects of motion sickness medicine the paratroopers had been given. Many of the scattered paratroopers, however, banded together and set off toward their assigned objectives.

Amazingly, the very scattering of the paratroop forces proved to be an asset to the Allies. Paratroopers were dropped so many places that the Germans had no idea where the major assault would come.

Three important objectives were captured by the ragged American paratroop forces in the early morning hours of June 6, 1944—the village of St. Mère Eglise, the

An American paratrooper patrol cautiously moves through a churchyard in St. Marcouf, behind the Utah Beach invasion area.

bridgeheads of the Douve and Meredet rivers, and the German barracks at Pouppeville. The capture of St. Mère Eglise was essential. National Route 13 would thus be available to the Allied troops, and inaccessible to the German forces. Control of the bridges at the Meredet and Douve rivers was of similar importance, for if German troops and artillery could not move into the invasion area to contest the landing, the seaborne troops on the beaches certainly stood a better chance of success in their assault.

The roadway at Pouppeville was one of the principal routes inland from Utah beach, where seaborne assault troops would be landing later that morning. The Germans had set up some barracks at Pouppeville in a series of farm buildings along the road. Staff Sergeant Harrison Summers was assigned a force of fifteen unseasoned paratroopers who had not before been in battle. He was ordered to take the barracks. The feat was accomplished through the courage and valor of Sergeant Harrison and one of the men under his command, Private John Carrier. Largely on their own, the two men secured the buildings, killing or capturing all the German defenders. The area secure, Sergeant Harrison spotted a tank coming up the road—a tank emblazoned with the orange recognition panel of the Allied forces. The first troops from the beach assault were traveling inland, and linking up with their airborne comrades.

3

THE INVASION BEGINS

When the order to shove off was finally given, many thousands of men aboard the more than six thousand ships—of all descriptions, from converted liners down to tank landing craft—bobbing in the English coastal waters had been waiting to disembark for over three days. Understandably nervous, and often seasick, the men had passed the time playing cards, writing letters home, or simply staring at the ceiling above their bunks. They knew that their mission was a difficult one, that despite the support of many combat ships that would be shelling the shore in advance of the landing, there would be many deaths, and many more casualties.

At the order to go, the troops climbed into thousands of landing craft and amphibious vehicles. At a central point out of the range of the German shore batteries, they regrouped into "waves." This concentra-

tion zone had been nicknamed "Picadilly Circus," for once there the landing craft were to travel in a circular holding pattern that bore a striking resemblance to the traffic pattern of that noisy London landmark.

The landing craft marked time until their scheduled moments of departure, when they wheeled out of the circle and headed in towards shore. They were to travel down specially marked "lanes," which had earlier been cleared of mines by minesweepers of the U.S. and Royal Navies.

For the invasion troops, the first danger of the landing was during the transfer from the large troopships to the small LCVP's (Landing Craft, Vehicle, Personnel). Each LCVP carried about thirty men standing up; seats had been deemed a luxury unnecessary in a combat craft. The men boarded the LCVP's by climbing down rope ladders hanging over the sides of the troopships. This descent was very dangerous, because the sea was rough, and the landing craft were small. If a soldier fell into the sea, he would probably drown,

GI's loading onto an LCVP prior to the invasion.

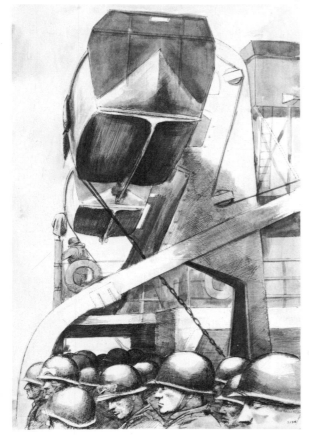

GI's wait aboard a large Navy troopship for the order to go. Above them hang LCVP's in lieu of lifeboats. The LCVP's were later lowered into the water and used for the invasion.

ships, cruisers, destroyers, and corvettes of the bombardment force saturated the beach area with heavy shelling. This bombardment would provide "cover" for the landing troops, enabling them to get ashore by forcing the German troops to remain in their shelters.

At precisely 6:30 A.M., on schedule to the minute, the first LCVP's scraped up against the beach. Soldiers scrambled ashore and sent up the black smoke signals that alerted the Navy to cease shelling the beach, for from that time on Allied troops would be endangered by the bombardment. The shelling would continue, but further inland.

Utah Beach was almost one kilometer wide, with a row of dunes behind it. Among these dunes lurked hundreds of German soldiers in dugouts and concrete "pillboxes." Behind these fortified dunes was a large meadow that had been flooded by the Germans to hinder an assault, one of the same meadows that had caused such difficulty for the airborne troops.

When the men reached the relative safety of the four-foot seawall behind the dunes, many of them were confused. The landmarks they were supposed to look for, a windmill and a particularly high set of dunes at de Varreville, were nowhere to be seen. It was General Theodore Roosevelt, Jr. (commanding officer for the Utah Beach invasion and a son of former President Theodore Roosevelt) who discovered—when reconnoitering the beach, moments after landing—that they had hit the beach a mile south of their target landing zone. General Roosevelt acted quickly, communicating with the waves of troops not yet

dragged beneath the water by the weight of his equipment. And a man might be crushed between the LCVP and the troopship, if a swell in the water caused either or both of the craft to move suddenly during his descent. Fortunately, during the entire operation few men suffered this fate.

At 4:55 A.M., the first wave of LCVP's detached itself from the group and started the ninety-minute journey to Utah Beach. They were led by patrol boats and radar craft. As the landing craft approached the shore, the British and American battle-

Bright rockets light up the sky during the pre-dawn naval bombardment of the entrenched German positions.

ashore to ensure that they would also land at the new site. Otherwise, the soldiers who had already landed would have been stranded alone on the beachhead.

All the while the American troops were landing, German heavy artillery shells were now falling on the beach, wreaking havoc among the invaders. Most of the shelling was coming from heavy batteries five miles to the south, on the other side of the river Dives.

Nevertheless, due in great measure to the success of the airborne troops, who had managed to cut off German communications and transportation behind the front

line, the invasion troops on Utah encountered minimal resistance. By 10 A.M., the seaborne troops had taken the beach and had met up with the first of the airborne troops near the targeted "Exit One," at the village of Pouppeville.

By midday, the battalion had captured and crossed the marshlands, and had linked up with airborne troops engaged in heavy fighting inland. On the whole, the invasion at Utah Beach had been easier than the strategic staff—or the troops—had expected.

Half an hour after the American assault began on Utah Beach, the British and Canadian forces began their assault on

Assault troops peer over the protective front of the landing craft as they approach the French coast.

Gold, Juno, and Sword beaches. There the German defenders did not prove much of an adversary.

The 716th German Infantry, an inferior force, consisted largely of soldiers under the age of seventeen or over the age of thirty-five, soldiers who had been badly wounded in conflict with Russian troops (many of them victims of third-degree frostbite), and soldiers who had been deemed otherwise unfit for the intense and desperate fighting German troops were engaged in on the Eastern Front. Hindered not only by inexperience and injury, these troops also suffered from a severe lack of motorized transportation. Each unit had one automobile for its commander, and one unit was equipped with bicycles. But these *bodenstandige*, or "static troops," were primarily intended to defend a fixed position until they were relieved by more mobile reinforcements from the Panzers.

German defense on Juno, Sword, and Gold beaches relied primarily on fixed-position artillery emplacements—large, cannon-like guns with a very small range of fire. Once these emplacements were knocked out by invasion troops, whether the guns were destroyed or the personnel killed, wounded, or captured, the area would be virtually defenseless, and could easily be overrun by Allied assault troops. However, most of these heavily fortified guns had survived the intense naval bombardment during the two hours before the invasion, although it had been the largest naval bombardment in the history of warfare. These guns were the major hindrance to the invading troops.

"Funnies"

The British had developed a series of specialized tanks to deal with the problems of this particular invasion. These tanks were called "funny tanks," or "funnies." There were a variety of different types, each designed for a specific invasion task: DD's, flails, bobbins, fascines, roly-polys, petards, crocodiles, self-propelled ramps, and bridging tanks.

The DD's—dual drive tanks—were the only funny tanks the Americans had decided to use. The DD was designed to "swim" in the water (aided by a propeller and kept afloat by a canvas screen supported by struts), and to crawl on land with a conventional track drive. Unfortunately, the vast majority of these tanks sank in the rough seas on D-Day, often drowning the men inside them.

Flail tanks were used to clear paths through German minefields. An ordinary Sherman tank with two arms attached to the front, between which was suspended a rotating drum with chains attached, these tanks "flailed" the ground in front of them, detonating any mines in their path without damage to the tank itself. These flail tanks left a wide, easily visible trail in the sands behind them, which the landing infantry troops followed to safety.

Bobbins and Roly-Polys were designed to lay makeshift roads of steel mesh matting across the soft dunes and slick patches of clay. Fascines carried huge bundles of logs, to be dumped in anti-tank ditches, filling them up and allowing the other tanks that followed to cross these traps in safety.

Self-Propelled Ramps were turretless tanks that, when parked beneath a seawall, formed a ramp that other tanks could use to pass over the wall. Bridging Tanks carried thirty-foot bridges that could be laid over obstacles and ditches, allowing

GI's help the survivors who made it safely to shore in an inflatable rubber raft.

troops and equipment to pass over them and on to the interior of the landing site.

Petard and Crocodile tanks were designed to destroy fixed gun emplacements. Petards were short-muzzled tanks that threw shells large enough to break through the concrete emplacements in which these large guns were housed. Crocodile tanks were designed to throw liquid fire—a much hotter flame, and from a much longer range than the infantry-carried flame throwers. They were used to clear German troops from their pillboxes (concrete gun emplacements). Although the funny tanks were enormously useful for their

A Navy demolition crew, among the first sent ashore, works under heavy fire to explode, disarm, and clear away the deadly obstacles placed by the German forces in the shallow coastal waters.

particular tasks, they proved to be even more effective when used in conventional roles as armored fighting vehicles.

Gold Beach

Gold Beach was a straight expanse of firm sand, approximately three miles long. There were small seaside villages at either end, Le Hamel on the west, La Riviere on the east. Behind Le Hamel rose a line of hills ending in seaside cliffs at the little village of Arromanches. Beyond La Riviere was a very high concrete seawall with a road running along the top of it. Between the two villages were dunes, with a strip of marshy land behind them. Beyond the marsh was a road that connected the two villages, and behind that road was a series of grassy hills in which a number of German heavy artillery batteries had been placed.

The invasion of Gold Beach did not prove to be as difficult as expected, overall, but at the western end of the beach, near Le Hamel, the invasion forces encountered stiff resistance. Here the British troops encountered the tough German 352nd Infantry Division, the same unit that would wreak havoc on the American troops at Omaha Beach. The German guns at this troublesome end of the beach were fixed on positions not out to sea, but along the high-water line on the beach. Thus, as the British soldiers waded ashore there, they came under direct, heavy, German fire. There were many casualties.

But if there was peril on Gold Beach, there was heroism, too. Company Sergeant Major H.W. Bowers, having survived the brutal artillery fire on the beachhead, identified its source—a pillbox (fortified gun emplacement) built into a sanitarium overlooking the beach. Bowers and two comrades managed to creep up on the big guns, fighting off the German patrols along the way. As his two comrades fired at any openings they could find, Bowers climbed onto the flat roof of the pillbox and dropped a grenade inside. The German gunners ran out, their hands in the air. A major source of the heavy fire on the beachhead was eliminated.

Juno Beach

On Juno Beach, the trouble began before the troops had waded ashore. There was a higher tide than had been expected, due to the poor weather, and it was rising fast. Therefore the German-placed beach obstacles—most of which were heavily mined—that were supposed to have been safely beyond the high water mark, making them easy to spot and to maneuver around, were below the water, and treacherous indeed. Many of the Allied LCVP's, very difficult to navigate because of their box-like construction, were destroyed by the mines. The wreckage accumulated along the water line, causing "traffic jams" among the vehicles and landing craft coming ashore. This made it difficult for successive incoming waves of troops and equipment to move inland up the beach.

The pre-invasion bombardment of Juno Beach, also intense, had been basically ineffective; afraid of bombing their own incoming troops, air force pilots had dropped their bombs too far inland. The German gun emplacements on Juno were virtually unharmed by the aerial bombardment, and the artillery fire faced by the Canadians on Juno Beach in the first minutes was devastating.

Since there was no line of protective hills behind Juno Beach for the Germans to hide in, German troops were stationed among the dunes and the houses of the seaside villages. Nevertheless, within fifteen minutes of the landing, the Canadian troops had managed to defeat and disarm this first line of German defense, in fierce fire fights, and even hand-to-hand combat.

As the wreckage was cleared from the beach, tanks and infantry were able to penetrate the villages of Courseulles and Berniers, which were taken without overwhelming resistance. The Canadians, however, ran into severe resistance in the orchards and meadows just beyond these villages, where they were held for several hours before pressing on to capture the largest territory covered by any invasion force that day.

Except for those first terrible minutes of battle—when men watched boats carrying their comrades explode and sink among the deadly beach obstacles, or watched their comrades die while struggling through the murderous German fire—the invasion at Juno Beach was by and large the most successful of all the D-Day invasions.

Sword Beach

Sword Beach was the most heavily fortified of the three "British" beaches. Ouistreham, just beyond it, was no seaside village, but a densely populated town that the Germans had fortified in order to protect the Caen Canal and the small port at the mouth of the Orne River. Although the paratroopers had captured the major gun battery at Merville, on the far side of the Orne port, and controlled the crucial bridges across the canal, the Germans had hidden mobile artillery in the forest around the invasion area. These guns, along with the fortified gun emplacements undamaged by the bombardment of Ouistreham, caused the invading British troops significant trouble.

Here, too, the invaders encountered trouble even before reaching the shore. The heavy seas swamped the vast majority of the DD tanks, and severely hindered the progress of the remaining few. Thus most of the infantry troops landed ahead of their armored support, rather than behind it as had been planned. The tanks were supposed to clear "lanes" up the width of the beach for the infantry to travel along in relative safety from beachhead mines.

As on the other beaches, wreckage became a problem, hindering the flails and other funnies hard at work to clear the beach of obstacles. The troops encountered heavy artillery fire from a strongpoint in the vicinity, at La Breche, which took three hours to subdue. It took a long time to secure Sword Beach, for the gun emplacements among the houses of the town had to be captured in close combat. And through it all the remarkably accurate long-range German guns continued to harass the soldiers coming up the beaches.

By midday, however, the seaborne troops at Sword Beach managed to break through, and rendezvous with the airborne troops holding the Caen Canal bridge. The invasion at Sword Beach was declared a success.

It was the inhabitants of Ouistreham who suffered the most during the invasion of Sword Beach. All but 400 of the 4000 inhabitants of the town had been evacuated to relative safety farther inland. But the town itself was virtually destroyed by the bombing and bombardment, or during the destructive infantry fighting between the invasion forces and German troops that went on from house to house in the town. Of the 400 inhabitants who had remained in Ouistreham, nearly a third were killed or wounded.

Deception Plan

The invasion at Utah, Gold, Juno, and Sword beaches was remarkably successful. This was partially due to the planning and coordination that had gone into the invasion, partially due to the bravery and determination of the men of the invasion forces. But another, perhaps even more important factor cannot be overlooked— the success of the deception plan, which had convinced the Germans that the Allied forces would land elsewhere, at the Pas de Calais.

For though the German gun emplacements did impede the invading troops, and though there were a few isolated units of first-line German soldiers entrenched there who gave the Allies a good deal of trouble, for the most part the German defense was a weak one. Hitler's best troops, and the bulk of the German materiel—heavy artillery, tanks, jeeps, etc.—were not in Normandy at all, but far away, across the Channel from the phony barracks and phony equipment the Allies had set up elsewhere in England. The Allied plan of deception had worked brilliantly.

The beachhead successes provided the invasion troops with another important weapon, one which would stand them in good stead as they traveled inland to further encounters with the defenders of Hitler's "Fortress Europe," the ramparts of

Troops rally behind a concrete seawall at Utah Beach before going over the top to take the interior.

which were these beaches of the French Coast. That weapon was confidence. Up to the time of the invasion, German troops had been markedly successful against the soldiers of the Allied armies. Even when losing, the Germans had fought doggedly and efficiently, consistently inflicting more damage on their enemies than they themselves sustained. The victories on the beaches of France, therefore, provided the Allied soldiers with a sense of confidence that was crucial to their continued success.

A major factor in Allied victories on Utah, Gold, Juno, and Sword beaches was the successful paratroop invasion of the night before. Although the casualties were severe, the paratroopers successfully broke off the German lines of communication and supply, as well as seriously distracting

and confusing German troops.

The terrain had been another factor in the Allied success on these beaches. On the whole these four beaches were relatively flat, with firm sands that provided easy access to the German gun emplacements. This allowed the Allied troops to quickly move off and beyond the beaches, and gain the precious toehold on the European continent that was to determine the outcome of the war.

By contrast, at Omaha Beach, the second of the American invasion zones, the terrain caused tremendous difficulties for the assault troops. Unlike Utah, Gold, Juno, and Sword, Omaha Beach was overhung with steep cliffs, along which were hidden large German guns that proved difficult to disable.

"BLOODY OMAHA" AND POINTE DU HOC

The invasion at Omaha Beach was by far the most difficult of those that took place along the northern coast of France on D-Day. The first problem the Allied armies encountered was caused by the weather.

The thick fog that had caused problems during the paratroop drops was the culprit here as well. The pilots of Allied bombers, out of concern that they might mistakenly bomb their own troops, dropped their bombs too far inland, and missed the fortified German gun emplacements along the beach. These guns, almost unscathed when the soldiers began landing on the beachhead, were the cause of hundreds of casualties. The aerial bombardment that was to have "neutralized" the German artillery had failed almost completely.

Omaha Beach was also physically the most hazardous of all of the invasion beaches. The six thousand yards of firm

Naval shelling of Omaha Beach as the invasion got underway. In the background the high bluffs directly behind the beach.

sand were backed by a line of steep hills, and cliffs that rose two hundred feet or more above the beach, along the top of which ran a high seawall. There were only five possible exits inland from the shore, along the gullies and dry stream beds that ran down to the sea. Each of these was defended by an entrenched German gun position. Also, as the beach was relatively exposed to the open seas, the Allied troops encountered difficulties landing, for the offshore waters were quite rough.

Omaha Beach was defended not by the *bodenstandige* of the 716th German Division, but by the seasoned troops of the 352nd German Division, which had been moved into the area immediately prior to the invasion, a fact of which the Allied command was unaware. These troops, of which there were eight battalions—a force twice as large as the Allies expected—proved to be very nearly fatal to the Allied armies. Entrenched as they were in a remarkably well-fortified defensive position, where even the terrain provided an advantage, these veteran German troops made the Allied forces pay heavily for every inch of Omaha Beach.

These were the conditions the American troops had to contend with at the Omaha beachhead on the morning of June 6, 1944. The rough waters caused the first problems for the landing troops. At least 10 LCVP's were swamped by the waves offshore, drowning many of the heavily-laden soldiers before they even had a chance to fight. The DD tanks were launched farther offshore than planned, with the result that twenty-seven of the thirty-two DD's sank like stones. More often than not, the men trapped inside the DD's drowned before they could escape. Here, too, therefore, infantry troops landed ahead of the armored support that was to have

created safe lanes through the minefields by which they could travel up the expanse of the beach.

Major-General L.T. Gerow, commander of the Omaha beach assault, had declined the use of all funny tanks except for the DD's. Although the use of funnies would probably not have changed the nature of the battle at Omaha Beach, it would have facilitated the beach landing somewhat. For as it was, soldiers—under heavy enemy gunfire—had to perform many of the tasks, such as clearing mines, for which the funny tanks had been designed.

As on the other beaches, LCVP's at Omaha were wrecked on beach obstacles submerged in the unusually high tide. Although they greatly hindered the progress of subsequent waves of invasion for-

GI's wade toward shore. Note the lack of cover from the withering gunfire strafing the beach.

Above, a wet and weary GI carries a full load of equipment ashore at Omaha Beach. Landing craft, in the background, jams the harbor. Below, medics administer a plasma transfusion to a wounded soldier on the beach.

ces, these wrecked LCVP's were a boon to the soldiers in the first wave, as they gave the men some small measure of shelter from the rain of heavy gunfire that covered the beach. At Omaha, the German guns were trained on the high water mark, and thus many landing soldiers were killed or wounded in their first moments ashore.

Lieutenant-General Omar N. Bradley, floating in the command ship offshore, was frustrated by the lack of communication with the forces on the beach. "Though we could see it dimly through the haze," said General Bradley, "and hear the echo of its guns, the battle belonged that morning to the thin, wet line of khaki that dragged itself ashore."

Of those soldiers who made it to the relative safety of the base of the cliffs, many were in a state of shock. The long, often seasick hours spent in the ships, and the trauma of surviving the landing, proved too much for some of the inexperienced soldiers. The casualty rate among officers was even significantly higher than among the soldiers. The cohesion of many units was destroyed by the confusion, and the heavy casualties sustained in the first moments of the landing.

One of the most difficult things in the course of a battle is leading men into the lethal hail of gunfire against all their instincts and better judgment. It is the job of the officers and more experienced troops to keep the momentum of battle going,

A lone medic moves along the narrow strip of beach below the chalk cliff, administering first aid to men who made it to safety.

and to lead the frightened and inexperienced into the heat of battle.

Many officers had been killed on the beach, and the vast majority of the troops at Omaha were "green," that is, they had never before been on the field of battle. Among the officers who remained, many lacked battle experience essential to effective leadership. The seasoned First Division of the United States Army, nicknamed "The Big Red One," was largely responsible for rallying the panicked troops on Omaha Beach and leading them on. On Omaha Beach, as in many situations where survival is at stake, the actions of a few individuals in many units who took matters into their own hands regardless of the odds were an inspiration to their comrades.

As the morning wore on, small groups of men managed to begin scaling the cliffs at Omaha Beach, and moving against the deadly gun emplacements. The Navy's destroyers gave strong support, often coming in as close as eight hundred yards from shore to fire at the heavily fortified German big guns. Largely responsible for beginning the movement up the hillside were Brigadier-General Norman B. Cota (who remarkably survived the hail of gunfire even while marching up and down the beach in blatant defiance of the dangers), and his staff officer, Major William Bretton. Cota stalked the beach, roaring orders at frightened troops. They then began to inch their way through the heavy gunfire, and small gains were made against the Germans. One by one the German guns fell silent, often the result of the actions of a few brave men who banded together to storm a battery with no thought for their

Medics treat the wounded, as the troops rest beneath the cliff face at Omaha. Below, the next wave of American assault troops cross the wreckage-strewn beachhead.

Omaha Beach shortly after the invasion. The rapid accumulation of wreckage hindered the movement of men and materiel into the invasion area. Below, these big landing ships were the primary mode of transport for heavy motorized equipment such as tanks, jeeps, trucks, and armored bulldozers on D-Day.

Dwight David Eisenhower

Dwight David Eisenhower was born in 1890 in Dennison, Texas. The family settled in Abilene, Kansas where "Ike" and his five brothers were raised. In order to gain the college education that he could not afford, Ike secured an appointment to the United States Military Academy at West Point. After his graduation in 1915, he married Mamie Geneva Doud. The outbreak of World War I led to Ike's assignment to Camp Colt in Gettysburg, Pennsylvania, where he trained the newly-formed tank troops and was soon made commanding officer. It was his talent for teaching and training which kept him, much to his dismay, out of active service for the duration of the war. He was stationed in the Panama Canal Zone from 1922 to 1924, and it was there that he worked closely with Brigadier General Fox Connor, who taught Eisenhower a great deal about military and political history. In 1933, Eisenhower was assigned to the Philippines where he served under General Douglas A. MacArthur. Eisenhower, convinced that an air force was crucial to Philippine security, learned to fly a plane during his investigation into the practical aspects of establishing such a force.

At the outbreak of World War II, Dwight D. Eisenhower had served in the United States Army for twenty-five years. He had spent ten of those years intimately involved with the troops, training and teaching them, while developing the rapport with and sympathy for the American soldier that were the hallmarks of his military leadership. Five years were spent in advanced study and officer training, and the ten years prior to the war involved with global policies of the military high command.

During the summer of 1941, Eisenhower distinguished himself leading the large-scale military exercises in California. Quicky promoted to Chief of Staff for the Third Army, and then to Chief of Operations at Washington, D.C., Ike saw his dreams of leading troops into battle fading. When the United States entered the war in Europe, Eisenhower was named U.S. Commander of the European Theater of Operations. After commanding the invasions of North Africa, Sicily and Italy, he was named Supreme Commander of the Allied Forces in Europe, and he led the D-Day invasion in that capacity.

In December, 1945, Ike became one of the only five men ever to achieve the rank of General of the Army, and he was placed in command of the occupation forces in Europe. That year he was also named Chief of Staff of the U.S. Army, where he worked to unify the branches of the armed forces and establish universal military training.

In 1948, Eisenhower resigned as Chief of Staff to become president of Columbia University, but returned to the Army in 1950 in order to help organize the North Atlantic Treaty Organization (NATO).

In 1952, Eisenhower resigned from the army to run for the presidency of the United States. His popularity as a World War II hero, and his promise to end the War in Korea, won him an easy victory over opponent Adlai E. Stevenson. The armistice in Korea was signed in 1953, although Eisenhower carried on a foreign policy of Communist containment. Re-elected in 1956, Eisenhower worked during his second term for civil rights legislation. In 1957, he sent federal troops to Little Rock, Arkansas, to enforce court-ordered school desegregation. He successfully moved through Congress the Civil Rights Acts of 1957 and 1960, and eliminated discriminatory practices in federal facilities and the District of Columbia.

As Cold War tensions mounted, the Eisenhower Doctrine, which declared that the United States would give military and economic aid to any Middle Eastern nation requesting it in order to reduce the threat of communist aggression in the area, was drafted. The United States Marines were sent to Lebanon in 1958. In 1961, tensions with Cuba escalated to the point that the United States broke off diplomatic relations.

The qualities of justice, leadership and identification with the average individual distinguished Dwight D. Eisenhower as both president and military commander.

A thin line of Rangers, outlined against the edge of the cliff at Pointe du Hoc. Upon capturing the gun emplacement visible on the right, they found that the big guns had been dismantled and moved.

own safety but rather for that of others, and for the success of the invasion.

Once their artillery was silenced, the German defenders could not for long hold off the Allied invasion force. Even though these Nazi troops possessed the ability to impede and confuse the Allied troops, and to inflict heavy casualties, they were so greatly outnumbered that an eventual Allied victory was inevitable.

Omaha Beach

As the first LCVP's struck out for Omaha Beach, a force of troops trained for another D-Day mission headed out on their own. The U.S. Army Rangers, a newly-formed special force, were preparing to take the German battery of heavy artillery pieces on the cliffs of Pointe du Hoc, a mile south of Omaha Beach. These huge 155mm guns, perched atop a 177-foot cliff that rendered them practically impregnable, were generally believed to be the most

dangerous of the German batteries, commanding the entire area of Omaha Beach.

The plan was for two hundred men of the crack 2nd U.S. Ranger Battalion to scale the cliffs and take the gun emplacements. The safety margin was slim indeed, for the men were virtually defenseless during their ascent. As one American General put it, "Three old ladies with brooms could defend that cliff."

While the Navy fired at the visible defenders on the top of the cliff, the Rangers approached the cliff base in amphibious landing vehicles, and raised extension ladders borrowed from the London Fire Brigade. As the Rangers atop the ladders attempted to cover their comrades, who were taking to the cliffs with bayonets and toggle ropes, the German soldiers rained rifle and machine-gun fire down upon them all.

Against the odds, the Rangers prevailed and took the cliff. But when they arrived at the top, they found only six telephone poles and an empty concrete fortress. The big guns had been moved inland.

The Rangers hunted down the German troops and subdued them. Having secured the area, as planned, they waited for their reinforcements. The Rangers had lost radio contact, however, and and it was assumed that their mission had been a failure. The second wave, bobbing offshore, was re-routed to the landing at Omaha Beach, where it was hoped these seasoned, highly trained troops would be of help to the invaders.

The Rangers scouting the area at Pointe du Hoc found, hidden in the woods, four of the six guns—aimed to cover Omaha Beach. They destroyed these guns, rendering them useless by dropping hand grenades in the breeches (the parts of the guns where the ammunition is loaded in). They were unable to locate the other guns.

The Rangers then held their position at Pointe du Hoc, until the gap was closed between Utah and Omaha beaches, and the invasion troops were headed inland to relative safety. Their mission that day is considered one of the most daring and resourceful in the history of warfare. To this day, the Rangers are one of the elite units of the U.S. Army, and weeks of grueling supplementary training are required to qualify for membership in this crack infantry unit.

The bravery, courage, and determination of Allied soldiers on the beaches of Normandy on D-Day, June 6, 1944, cannot be overstated. The many months of planning, coordination, and training paid off handsomely on that day, paving the way for the Allied assault on Hitler's stronghold in Europe, and hastening the day when the people of Europe, including those in Germany, would be free of the evils of Nazism. Whatever the cost, it had been worth it.

These Rangers were awarded the Distinguished Service Cross for gallantry and heroism in action.

AFTERWORD

THE FALL OF "FORTRESS EUROPE"

By June 11, 1944, just five days after the invasion began, the Allies had consolidated a position on the Normandy coast of France that was almost eighty miles long and twenty miles in depth. With the overwhelming Allied air superiority, it was highly unlikely that the German Army would be able to dislodge them. The first phase of the campaign was over, though men and materiel (supplies), in vast numbers and quantities, continued to come ashore.

At the end of June, over one million Allied troops had arrived in France. This unprecedented accomplishment was the result of Allied ingenuity. Old merchant ships were sunk to create a sheltered anchorage, code named "Gooseberry." And concrete caissons (watertight, box-like chambers used in underwater construction) had

The severe storm of June 19-22 caused extensive damage to the floating piers.

been sunk to form two artificial harbors, code named Mulberry—an entirely new kind of structure specifically designed for this invasion. Though one of the Mulberries was destroyed in a storm, for a time the other made up for the lack of a usable harbor within the Allied-control zone. By the end of July, the Allies had conquered the French harbor city of Cherbourg, but the Germans had demolished its port facilities so thoroughly that it could not be used until late August.

Shortly after the invasion began, Hitler ordered that his secret weapon, the V-1—a pilotless aircraft powered by rockets and filled with explosives—be used to bomb London. Its use as a terror weapon was hard on British civilians. But Hitler did not use it against the invasion buildup areas in southern Britain (because Allied security had been so successful that the Germans were unaware of the location). Nor was the V-1 used against the Allied armies in Normandy itself.

In August, 1944, Hitler added the V-2 to his attack on London. A weapon even more terrifying than the V-1, the V-2 was a ballistic missile. It rose into the stratosphere and when it fell to earth it could not be seen or heard before it struck. This weapon was not used against the Allied invasion of Europe either. It, too, was used only as a terror weapon against the British civilian population, to frighten the British people, and to demoralize the British fighting forces abroad who would hear of the destruction at home. In the end, neither the V-1 nor the V-2 had any effect on the course of the invasion or the war.

Even if Hitler was still full of fight, his generals could see that the invading forces could not be held off indefinitely. Although in June they had been able, by military skill, to stabilize a fighting front and hold the Allied armies inside a relatively small area, the German High Command knew that the fourteen divisions they had in line would sooner or later be defeated by the ever-growing Allied troop concentrations.

The German generals wanted to retreat while there was still time, and then sue for peace on the best terms they could get. A fighting withdrawal across France, they felt, might wear down the Allies enough so that a compromise peace could be secured.

Hitler would have none of it. He refused to discuss retreat, or negotiations for peace, and he refused to prepare any fortified positions in France west of the German border.

A group of German generals made an attempt on Hitler's life on June 20, 1944. Many of Germany's best generals were implicated in the plot—which only failed because a heavy wooden table protected Hitler from the full effects of an exploding

A group of German troops and laborers are rounded up by two American soldiers. It was not uncommon for GIs, like the soldier in this picture, to continue to fight despite injuries.

A battalion of Engineers moves through the village of St. Lô, clearing this vital supply route of obstacles and mines. Below, inhabitants of St. Mère du Mont greet members of the 101st Airborne with smiles and bottles of wine in celebration of their liberation from German occupation.

Left, General Henry H. Arnold (left), commander of the U.S. Airborne troops, and Lieutenant General Omar N. Bradley, commander of the U.S. seaborne invasion troops, appear greatly relieved at the success of the risky operations. Above, Army and Navy chiefs visit French soil for the first time, June 12, 1944. Left to right, General Henry H. Arnold, Admiral Ernest King, General Dwight D. Eisenhower, and General George C. Marshall.

bomb. The only result of the attack was the deaths of many of Germany's best soldiers—including General Erwin Rommel, who was eventually forced to commit suicide for his part in the plot. Hitler was more powerful in Germany after the plot than he had been before. He would have to be defeated by fire and sword.

Breakthrough

Meanwhile, in Normandy, the battle raged. In the North was tank country—orchards, and flat open fields—where the British and Canadian armies faced the bulk of the German armored forces in a tough battle for Caen. The Germans held on grimly, but the battle consumed much of their best forces.

In the South, the hedgerow country had bogged down the American advance, which for a month could be computed in terms of yards rather than miles. The centuries-old "hedgerows," which grew atop thick dirt banks, bordered the fields of each farm. These hedgerows made a small fort of every little plot of land in the *bocage* country, as it was called. It was extremely difficult to maneuver tanks across this terrain.

At last, on July 26, 1944, the Americans broke out of the Normandy bottleneck. General Patton's Third Army, newly committed to the battle, roared through the gap created by the weary First Army, and the Battle of Normandy was over. The Battle of France had begun.

Now was the time for the Germans to retreat, before they were completely routed. But Hitler wouldn't hear of it. Instead, in August, on Hitler's orders, the Germany army counter-attacked.

Hitler wanted to cut the American forces in two. All he was able to do was to create a salient—a V-shaped angle in the line of confrontation. The Americans attacked it from the south at Argentan. The British and Canadian forces came down from the north toward Falaise.

Between August 16, and August 21, 1944, the German Panzers (armored divisions) were caught in the nutcracker of the Falaise-Argentan pocket. It was not quite closed, and many Germans escaped to fight another day. But the Allies captured over 50,000 prisoners, and killed or wounded as many more.

The German army streamed back across France with the Americans and British on

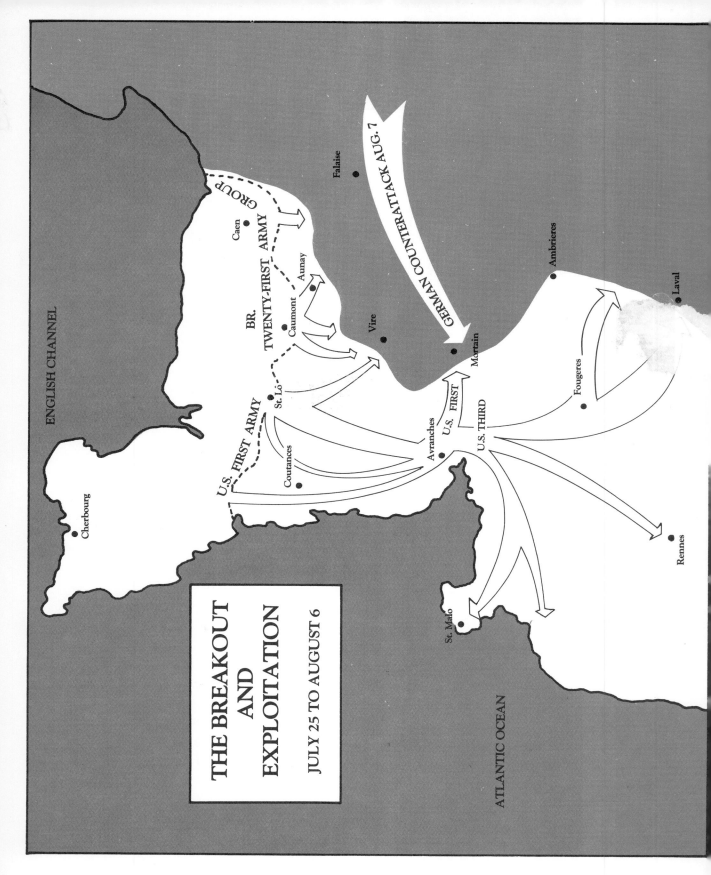

THE BREAKOUT
AND
EXPLOITATION
JULY 25 TO AUGUST 6

ENGLISH CHANNEL

ATLANTIC OCEAN

GERMAN COUNTERATTACK AUG. 7

BR. TWENTY-FIRST ARMY GROUP

U.S. FIRST ARMY

U.S. FIRST

U.S. THIRD

Cherbourg

Caen

Aunay

Caumont

St. Lô

Coutances

Vire

Falaise

Mortain

Avranches

St. Malo

Rennes

Fougeres

Ambrieres

Laval

Above, three Rino barges and a petrol barge are being hammered by the surf. Below, a jeep drives down the flexible floating roadway.

their heels. The advance of the Allies was only limited by the speed at which they could travel, and their ability to keep their forces supplied with fuel and the necessities of war.

On August 15, 1944, the Allies landed a second force in southern France. On August 25, 1944, the Free French (members of the French military forces who had refused to capitulate to Hitler in 1940) and the Americans liberated Paris.

By September, 1944, about 225,000 Allied soldiers had been killed, wounded, or captured. However, over 300,000 German soldiers had suffered similar fates, and 200,000 more were hopelessly bypassed in fortresses and cities of the remaining positions of Hitler's breached defense line on the French coast.

But the two million Allied soldiers advancing across the country—and the people of France, who, now that they had been liberated, had to be fed—were creating a terrific strain on logistics. The German soldiers in some of the port cities of France fought on fanatically under orders from Hitler to defend to the death, preventing Allied capture of additional ports. Some German-garrisoned French cities had been bypassed by the Allies—that is, the Allied forces had not attempted to capture them. Still others, like Brest, were totally destroyed in the fighting. Ahead of the Allies lay the German border and the Siegfried line—a long-standing fortified line of defenses behind which the Germans were rallying at last.

The Allies decided on an end run around the Germans in the North by means of a surprise armored-airborne

The huge caissons of the Mulberry harbors being constructed in the shipyards of Portsmouth in England. From here these massive concrete structures were floated across the Channel to be used as a breakwater.

assault across several rivers in Holland. Had it succeeded, it probably would have ended the war. But the Germans were able to defeat the over-ambitious Allied plan.

The Allied advance ground to a halt at the Siegfried line, having finally outrun its supply lines. A major port, such as Antwerp, had to be secured and repaired before a further advance could be launched.

Meanwhile, in the East, the Russian Red Army was moving forward. When Russian forces occupied land, they would not give it up. The line where the Russian Army and the American and British armies would finally meet would be the dividing line of the spheres of influence in postwar Europe, and thus the new front line for the modern world. Unless the Allies could somehow break the German border defenses, that line would be the border of France and Germany.

All through the fall of 1944, the Americans and the British fought their way into Hitler's Siegfried "West Wall." This was a land of forests and broken country, cleverly fortified by the Germans so as to keep any invader from German soil.

The Belgian port of Antwerp, captured by the Allies in September, was eventually cleared by December, and the Allied supplies began to build up again. Hitler knew that if he kept his armies behind their fortifications, he could hold the Allies off indefinitely. But dreams of victory still preoccupied his increasingly unbalanced mind. Hitler ordered that an attack by most of his remaining armored troops be made upon a thinly defended, "quiet" American sector, the Ardennes, during the dead of winter.

Hitler stripped his armies in the East of troops for this Ardennes offensive. He

"Sinking the Breakwater"—the enormous concrete caissons being sunk off the coast of France.

These landing platforms extending one thousand yards off Omaha Beach were enormously useful in facilitating the rapid movement of vast amounts of supplies and materiel into the invasion area.

would drive through the Allied lines and split the Americans from the British, take Antwerp, and dictate a peace. Then he would deal with the Russians.

Hitler's offensive began on December 16, 1944. The Americans fell back before the German *blitzkreig*. For a while it was 1940 all over again. The bad winter weather grounded American air forces. Some American units were routed, and totally defeated. Others, like the 101st Airborne Division at Bastogne, hung on grimly, though surrounded and bypassed by the major force of German attackers driving toward Antwerp.

To the North of the spearhead of the German attack, British and American forces under the leadership of British General Viscount Sir Bernard Law Montgomery were able to hold together against the German forces. Up from the South came General Patton's American tanks, roaring into the action. Patton had turned his

entire army around at a 90° angle in only thirty-five hours—an unprecedented feat of logistics. The German attack was blunted. The point of the German concentration became just another big salient, and the battle came to be called "the Battle of the Bulge."

The skies cleared, and the Allied air forces pounded the German tanks. Patton's forces relieved the gallant troops at Bastogne. In the West, the last German offensive of the war came grinding to a halt. Hitler threw in more and more troops, but by mid-January, 1945, the Bulge in the Ardennes was no more. The Allies had won. But they had lost 75,000 men. The Germans lost 125,000 men, and most of their remaining tanks and planes.

The Final Gasp

The German army was again in full retreat, largely abandoning their frontier defenses. German morale was collapsing. The Allied

EUROPE AFTER WORLD WAR II
THE IRON CURTAIN

bombers were reducing Germany to ashes. The handwriting was on the wall for Nazi Germany. In February, 1945, the Americans and the British moved up to the Rhine River in the West, and the Russians entered Germany from the East.

In desperation, the Germans blew up the dams in the Ruhr industrial region, and all the bridges on the Rhine. Miraculously, however, one Rhine bridge failed to fall. On March 7, 1945, the Americans crossed the Rhine at Remagen, and pierced into the heart of Germany.

Instead of rushing to Berlin, the Americans and the British cleared the Ruhr of German defenders. Meanwhile, the Russians took the remaining capitals of Eastern Europe, and Berlin itself.

The Allied troops met up with the Russian armed forces at Torgau, on April 25, 1945. On April 29, 1945, Hitler committed suicide.

On May 8, 1945, Germany surrendered. The German attempt to dominate Europe was finally at an end. On that date the world that we know came into existence—a world divided into two spheres of influence that included two separate Europes, divided by what Winston Churchill referred to a short time later as the "Iron Curtain." The era known as the "Cold War" between the Allied victors of World War II had begun.

Europe is divided still. American armed forces are still in Europe, defending the line of our armies' farthest advance in World War II.

We may question what we have won. We might try to second-guess those in command at the time, by saying to ourselves that the Allies should have invaded Germany sooner, and thus gotten a better jump on the Russians, so that more of Europe would today be "free." But regardless of whatever else might be said, it is indisputable that D-Day marked a turning point in the history of America—for D-Day was not only the start of the assault on Hitler's Fortress Europe, but also the beginning of contemporary American involvement in Europe. D-Day was a turning point, too, in the history of the world—the beginning of the end of the Nazi empire. Only after the war was the full extent of the horror of Nazi rule revealed—millions of noncombatants (Jews, gypsies, political dissenters, citizens of captured countries) had been lost to genocide, murder, or slave labor to the death. It is hoped that a lesson has been learned through the suffering of those millions, and that such a thing will never happen again. D-Day and its aftermath made it possible for the free peoples of the world to have a second chance. We owe it to the gallant men who fought to conquer the forces of Nazi Germany to use this chance to make a better world.

The cemetery at Normandy, where the brave men who were killed in the cause of the invasion are buried.

INDEX

Page numbers in *italics* indicate illustrations.

SUGGESTED READING

CALVOCORESSI, PETER and GUY WINT. *Total War: Causes and Courses of the Second World War.* New York: Penguin Books, 1979.

HASTINGS, MAX. *Overlord: D-Day and the Battle for Normandy.* New York: Simon and Schuster, 1984.

HORWARTH, DAVID. *D-Day: The Sixth of June, 1944.* New York: Pyramid Books, 1969.

JACKSON, W.G.F. *'Overlord': Normandy 1944.* Newark, Delaware: University of Delaware Press, 1978.

WILLMOTT, H.P. *June 1944.* Poole, Dorset, U.K.: Blandford Press, 1984.

1 2 3 4 5 6 7 8 9 10—JDL—95 94 93 92 91 90 89 88 87 86

940.54
MIL
    Miller, Marilyn
      D-Day

DATE DUE			